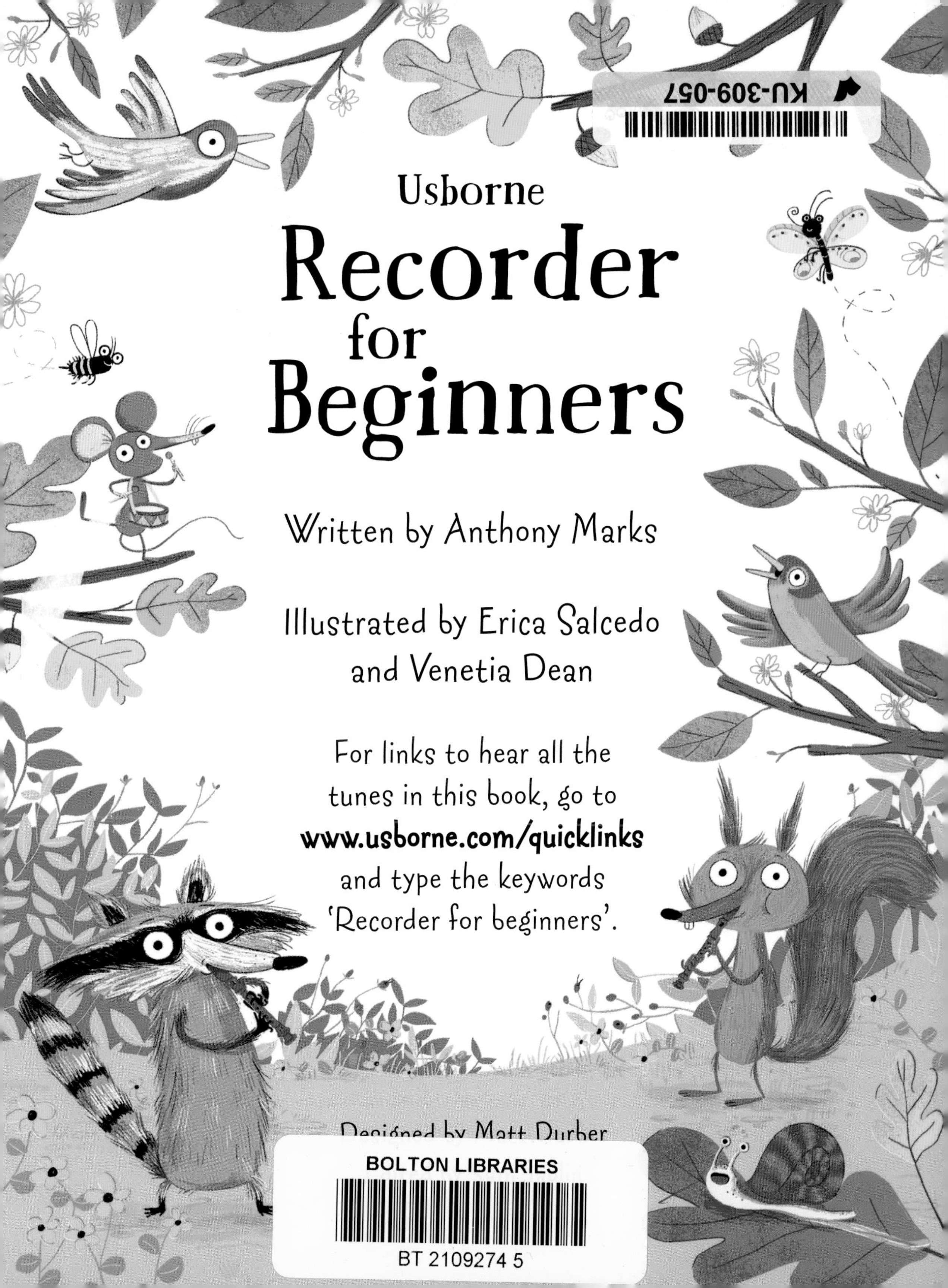

Usborne

Recorder for Beginners

Written by Anthony Marks

Illustrated by Erica Salcedo
and Venetia Dean

For links to hear all the
tunes in this book, go to
www.usborne.com/quicklinks
and type the keywords
'Recorder for beginners'.

Designed by Matt Durber

This book tells you how to have fun playing the recorder.

Read the first few pages to learn the basics, then start playing the tunes in the rest of the book.

Contents

Your recorder

Some recorders come in one piece, ready to play. Others come in three parts – head, middle and foot – that you put together before you play. Here's how to do this.

First, gently push and twist the **foot** part onto the thinner end of the **middle** part.

Then, gently push and twist the **head** part onto the other end of the **middle** part.

Your recorder should look like this:

Make the large **slot** in the head part line up with these **holes** in the middle.

Twist the little holes on the foot part so that they are turned slightly away from the holes on the middle part.

Getting ready to play

You can play your recorder standing up or sitting down. Make sure your back and shoulders are straight but relaxed.

If you sit on a chair, rest your feet on the floor.

Your feet should be slightly apart and your whole body should be relaxed.

Hold the recorder with your **left hand** at the top and your **right hand** lower down. Don't worry about covering the holes at first. Just hold it gently.

Your **left thumb** should be near the hole on the back, slightly bent at the knuckle.

Rest the recorder on your **right thumb**, opposite the fourth hole down.

Put the recorder to your mouth. Rest the tip on your bottom lip, then gently close your top lip onto it. Don't squeeze.

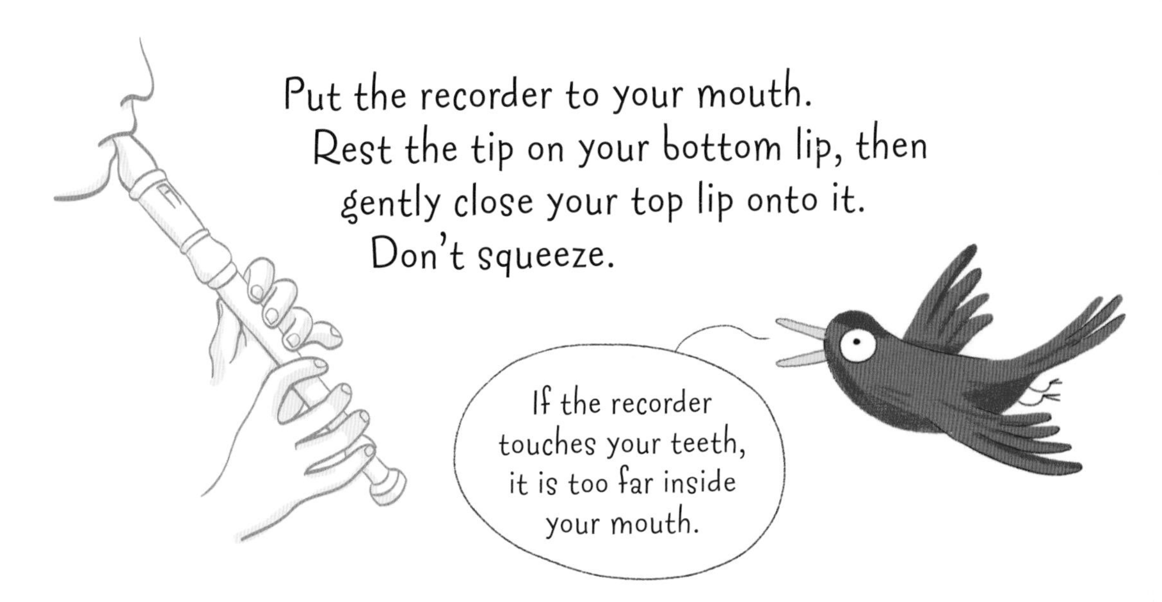

Without covering the holes, blow the recorder gently a few times and listen. Next, cover the **hole on the back** with your left thumb and the **top hole on the front** with the first finger of your left hand. Blow gently and listen again.

Each time you blow, say 'tuh'. There is more about this on the next page.

Your first notes

Musical sounds are called notes. Notes are named after the first seven letters of the alphabet. The note you played on page 5 is called B. Here it is again, with some more notes. Try playing them.

B

Cover the **thumb hole** and **top hole** as on page 5.

A

Like B, but cover the **second hole** down too, with the second finger of your left hand.

G

Like A, but cover the **third hole** down too, with the third finger.

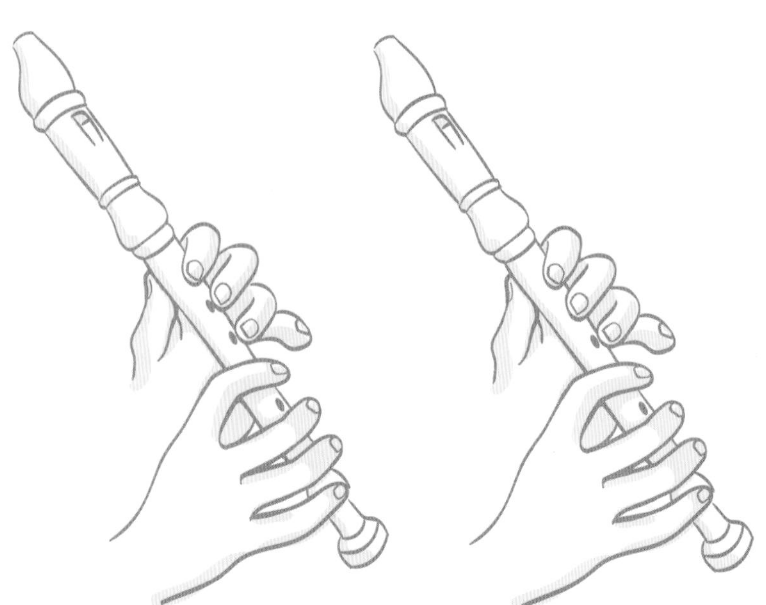

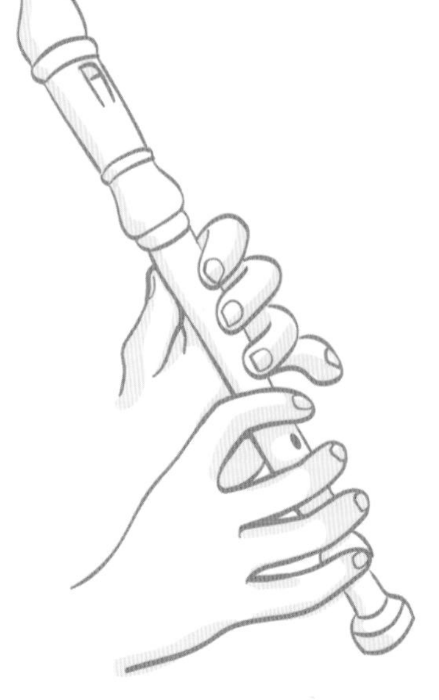

For these notes, you only need the fingers and thumb of your left hand.

Don't cover any holes with your right hand, but keep resting the recorder on your right thumb.

Play B, then A, then G a few times. Now play G, then A, then B.

Remember to say 'tuh' at the start of each note. This controls the flow of air and makes the notes sound neat.

In music, some sounds are higher and some are lower. When you play B, A, G, the sounds get lower one by one. When you play G, A, B, the sounds get higher.

Can you play two notes in a row to make a sound like a cuckoo? You need two notes out of B, A and G. Which ones?

Making notes into tunes

Can you play this 'button and string' tune? Each button shows a note. Play B for every button above the string, A for the buttons on the string, and G for the button below the string.

Make all the notes last the same amount of time.

Playing tunes

You can use B, A and G to play lots of tunes. In this book, patterns like the ones below show you where to put your fingers for each note. The circles show the holes on your recorder.

If the circle is black, cover its hole with the correct finger or thumb. If it is white, leave the hole uncovered.

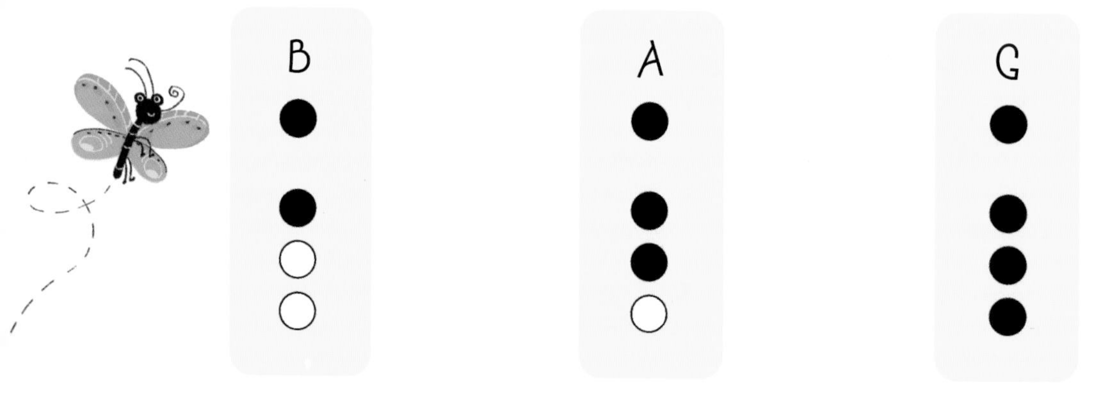

For B, cover the **thumbhole** with your left thumb, and the **first hole** with the first finger of your left hand.

Add the **second finger** of your left hand to play the note A ...

...and the **third finger** for G. (So three fingers in all, and your thumb too.)

For a reminder about how to hold your fingers and hands, look at page 6 again.

In music, some sounds are long and some are short. You measure the sounds by counting. Try counting '1, 2, 3, 4' out loud a few times. Then clap or tap along in time with the counting.

Make the clap or tap for '1' a bit louder than the rest.

Merrily we roll along

Now you can use the notes B, A and G to play a tune called 'Merrily we roll along.' The length of the shapes below shows you how many counts each note lasts for.

- Take a breath before you start to play.
- Count '1, 2, 3, 4' in your head as you play.
- Remember to say 'tuh' at the start of every note.
- Don't breathe before every note.
- Try to take a breath only when you see the ✓ sign.

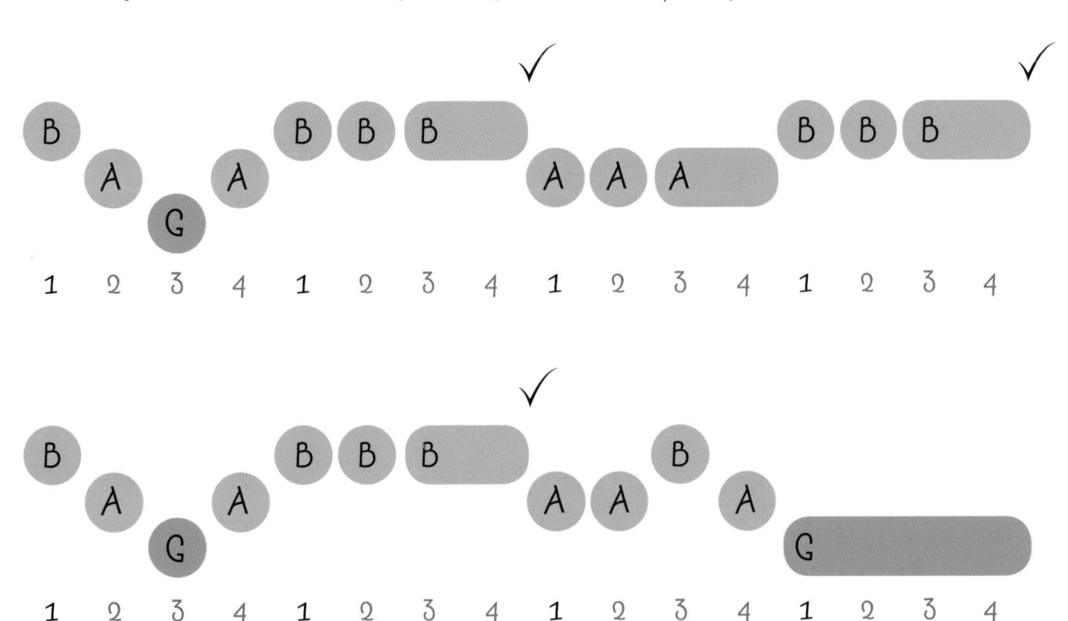

Writing music down

There is a special way of writing music down that helps you to play tunes made up by other people, and to write down your own tunes too.

Here is what 'Merrily we roll along' looks like written down.

- If you remember the tune, try playing it while looking at the music.
- The oval shapes are called note heads. The position of each one tells you how high or low each note is.

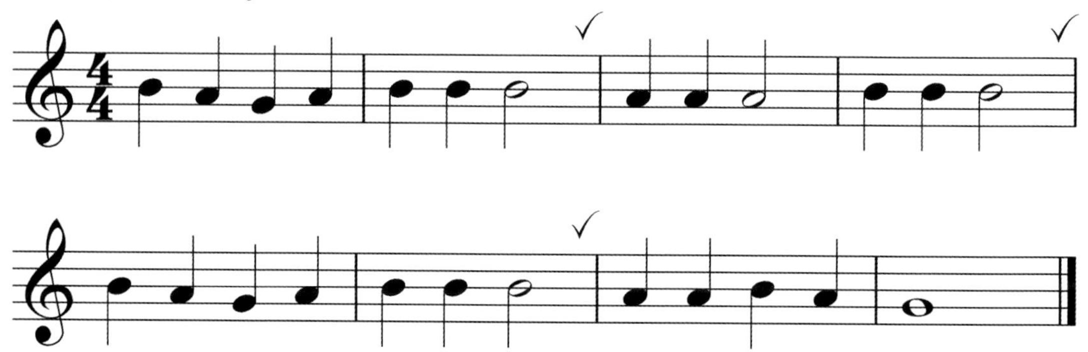

- Other things tell you how long notes last. Here's how it works:

A note with a black head and a stem lasts for **one count**.

A note with a hollow head and a stem lasts for **two counts**.

A hollow note head with no stem lasts for **four counts**.

Notes are written on a group of five lines called a staff or stave, either on the lines or in the spaces between them.

Now try playing 'Merrily we roll along' from the music. Don't forget to count, and to say 'tuh' at the start of each note.

Two new tunes

Opposite is the music for two new tunes using B, A and G. Here is a reminder of how to play the notes you need, and what they look like in music. Play them a few times.

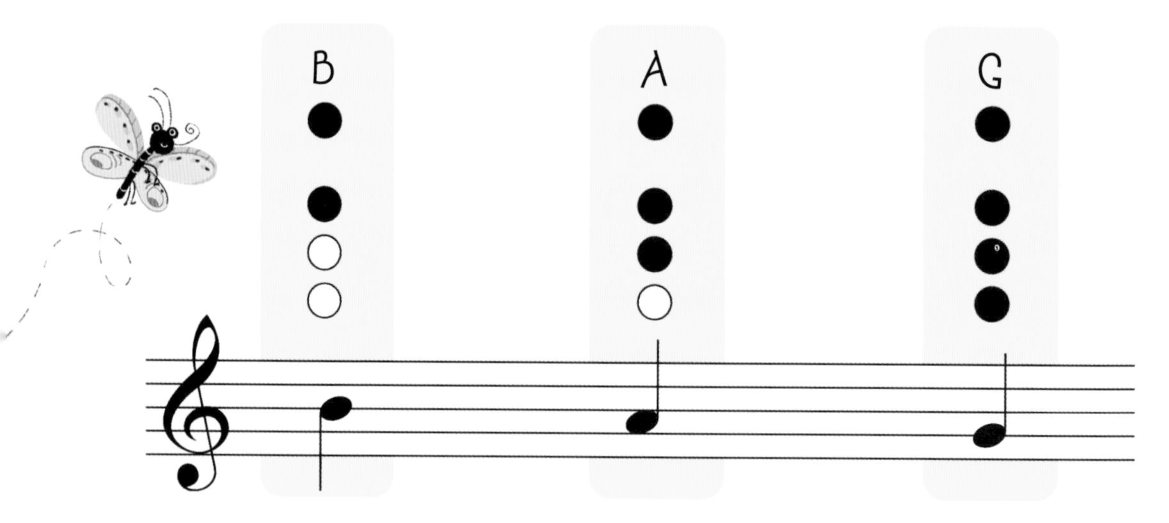

You count in groups of four for both tunes. Remember what notes of different lengths look like.

Go and tell Aunt Nancy

Count two bars in your head before you start. Take a breath on the last count so you are ready to play. Keep counting throughout the tune.

Au clair de la lune

The title of this song is French for 'In the moonlight'. Count a bit more slowly for this one, as it is more gentle.

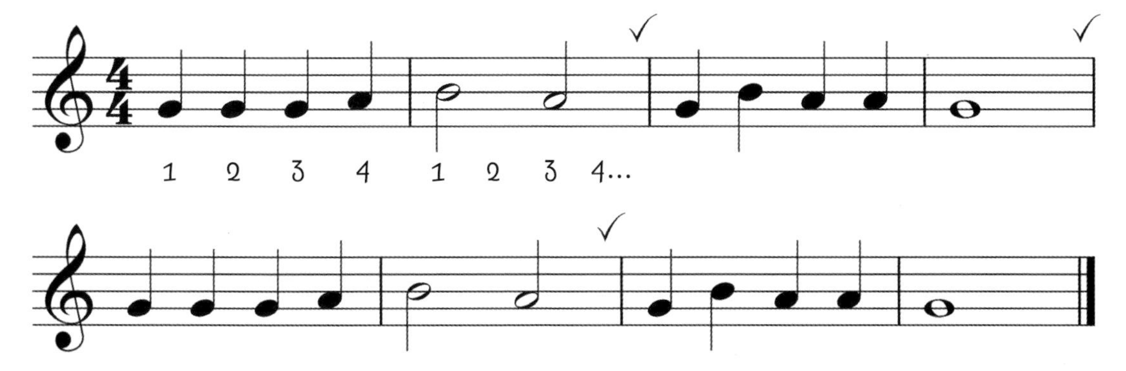

A new note: D

To play D, cover the second hole with the second finger of your left hand.

Here are the notes you have learned so far. You can use them to play 'Mary had a little lamb' on the opposite page.

Try moving from B to D and back again a few times before trying to play 'Mary had a little lamb'.

Mary had a little lamb

Count quite quickly when playing this tune. Remember to take a breath each time you see the ✓ sign.

Moving neatly between notes

As you learn more notes, you have to move your fingers more. If you find it tricky to move neatly between two notes, play them slowly a few times then speed up bit by bit.

- Always keep your fingers near the holes, even when you are not covering them.
- Don't waggle your fingers.
- Move your fingers gently and quickly, at the same time as you say 'tuh'.
- Remember to relax!

A new note: C

To play C, cover the second hole with the second finger of your left hand, and the thumbhole with your left thumb.

Don't cover any other holes.

Keep resting your recorder on your right thumb.

Here are all the notes you have learned so far. You can play lots of tunes with them. Use them for 'Lightly row' opposite, and all the tunes up to page 21 of this book.

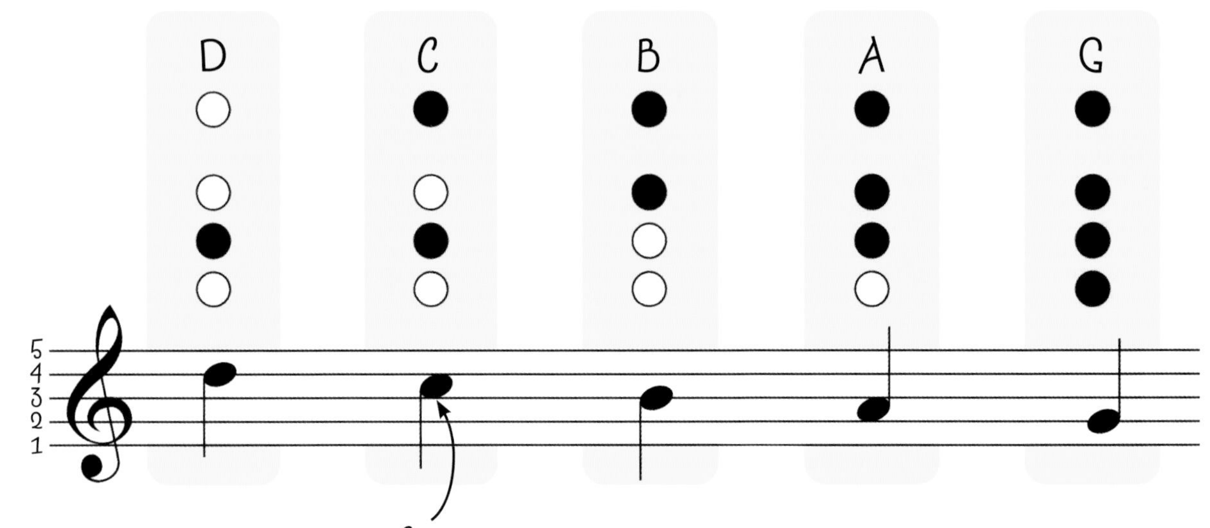

C sits between lines 3 and 4.

Play D, C, B, A, G. Can you hear the notes moving down by steps? Now play G D. Can you hear the big jump up from the low note to the higher one?

Lightly row

Make this tune sound lively and light.

Step, jump or the same?

Each tune has its own pattern of notes. Sometimes they move by steps, sometimes by jumps, and sometimes they stay the same.

Play these patterns from 'Lightly row' and listen carefully.

G A B C D

These five notes move up by step.

_ _ _ A G

A to G is a step down, as there is no note in between.

_ C _ A _

C to A is a jump down, as there is a note in between. Which?

G _ B _ D

These three notes move up by jumps.

D D D

These three notes stay the same.

D _ _ _ G

This is the biggest jump in the tune, down to the last note.

Can you find all these patterns in the music above? Try to play them without looking at the finger chart.

Counting in threes

The tunes you have learned so far in this book are all counted in groups of four, but not all music is like this. Sometimes you have to count in groups of three.

Each note still lasts for the same number of counts as on page 11, but when you are counting in threes, there are a few other things to remember.

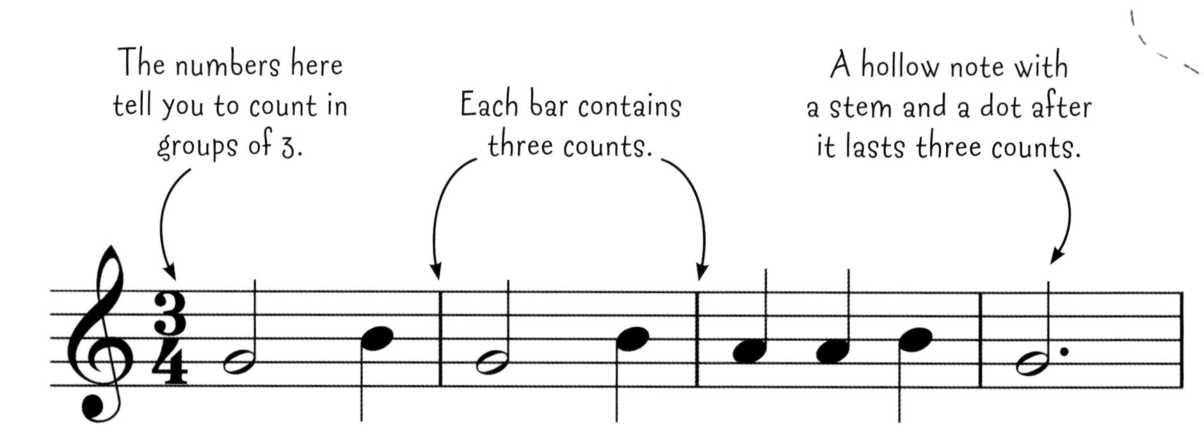

The cuckoo

Count two bars of three time in your head before you start to play this tune, and keep counting all the way through. Remember to say 'tuh' to start each note.

Can you hear the two different cuckoo sounds in this tune?

Shorter notes

Sometimes you have to play two shorter notes which add up to one count. In music, groups of two short notes are shown linked together by a line called a beam.

The tune below and the one opposite contain these short notes.

- Count regularly and play the two short notes in a single count.
- Say 'tuh' at the start of each note, even when they are short.

Pease pudding hot

It can help to think 'and' in between the two counts, like this.

When not to play notes

In some tunes, you don't play a note on every count of every bar. You have to leave a gap in the music. Special signs called rests tell you when to do this.

This sign tells you to rest for one count.

- Keep counting as usual but don't play anything.
- A rest is often a good place to take a breath.

The grand old duke of York

There are two one-count rests in this tune. For each one, just count regularly and don't play anything on count 3.

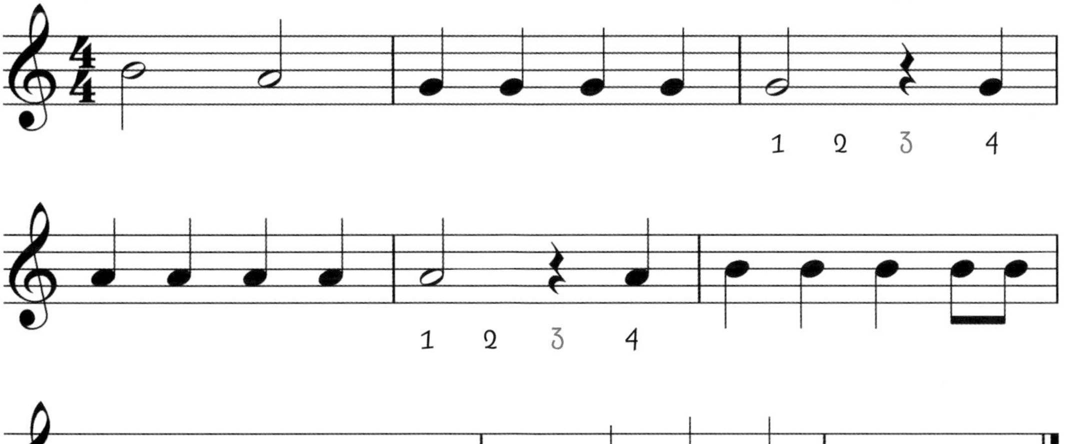

For short repeated notes, try saying 'tuh-kuh' instead of 'tuh-tuh'.

A note for the right hand

Now it's time to use your right hand to play a new note, low D. Cover all the holes on the recorder except the ones on the foot part.

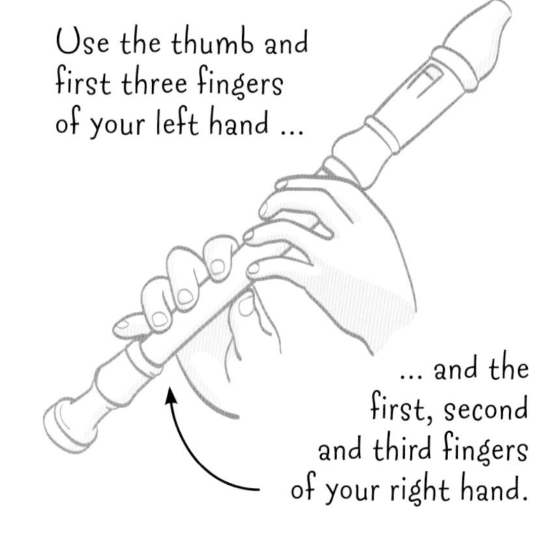

This chart shows the notes you already know, and the new one, low D. If a circle is black, cover that hole.

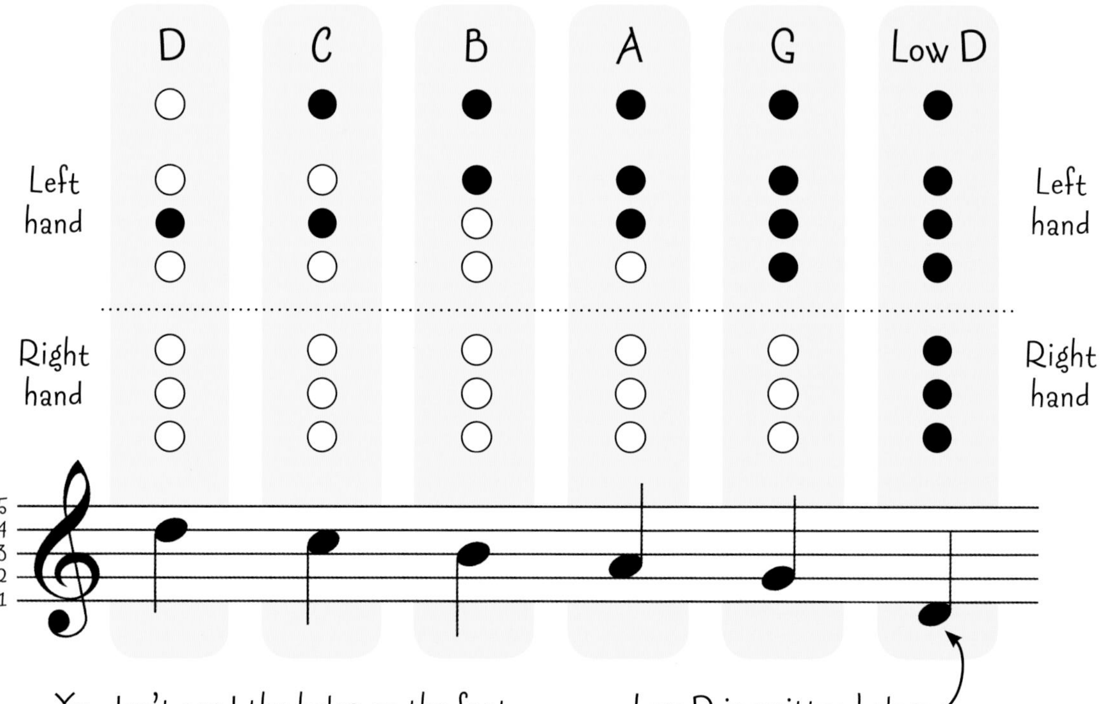

You don't need the holes on the foot part for any notes in this book.

Low D is written below the bottom line.

Playing low notes

Play D and low D a few times. Can you hear the big jump between them? Move your fingers quickly. For the low note, make sure you cover all the holes fully. Blow it gently or it will squeak.

Hot cross buns!

Now use all the notes you know to play 'Hot cross buns!'

- Play it slowly at first.
- When you can play all the notes, try it faster.

Another right-hand note: E

To play E, cover all the left-hand holes, and the top two right-hand holes with the first and second fingers of your right hand.

Keep your third finger near the holes.

Don't cover the holes on the foot part.

This chart shows the notes you already know, and the new one, E. With these notes, you can play all the tunes in the rest of the book.

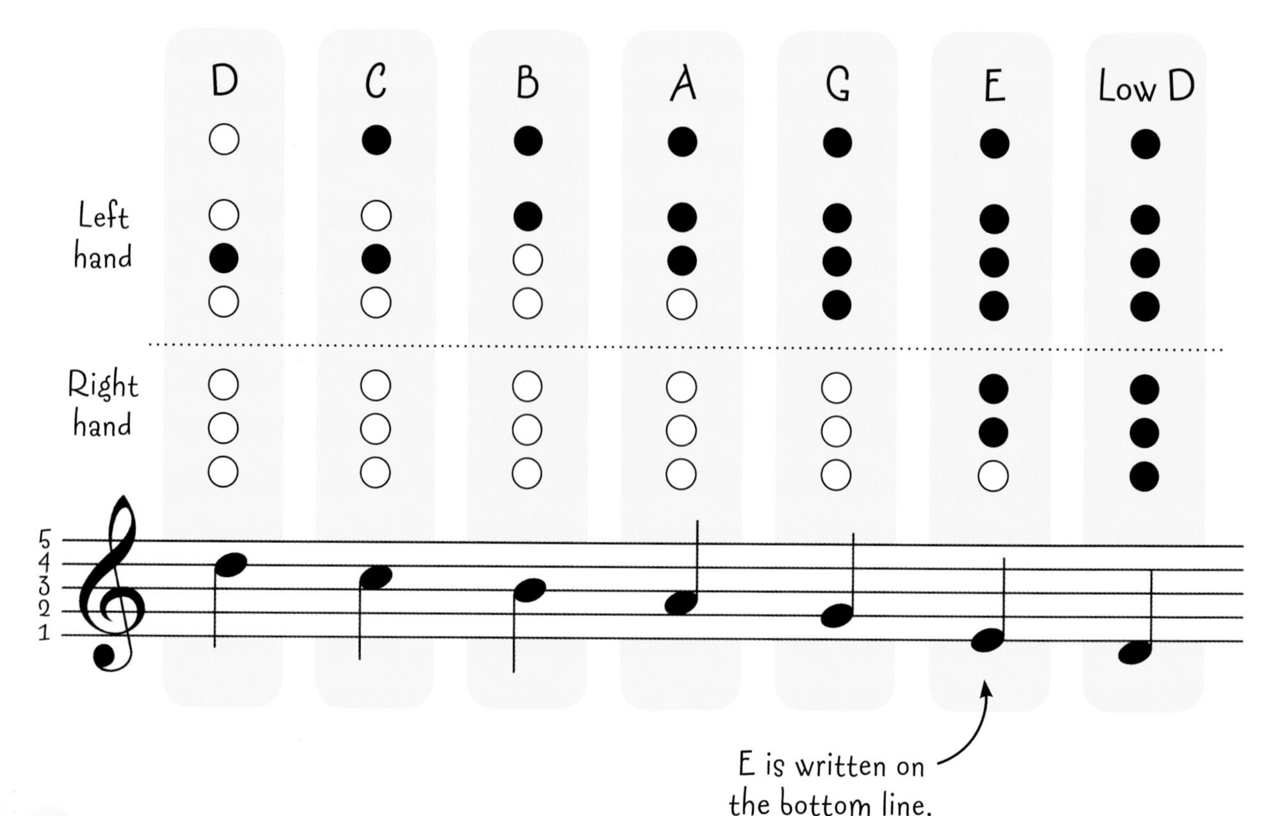

E is written on the bottom line.

Old MacDonald had a farm

Count quite quickly to make the tune sound lively. But don't start off too fast, or the short notes will be hard to play!

Learning new tunes

On the next few pages, you will find tunes to play using the notes you have learned.

Before you start to play a new tune, look carefully at the music. Try to imagine how it will sound. Can you hum it?

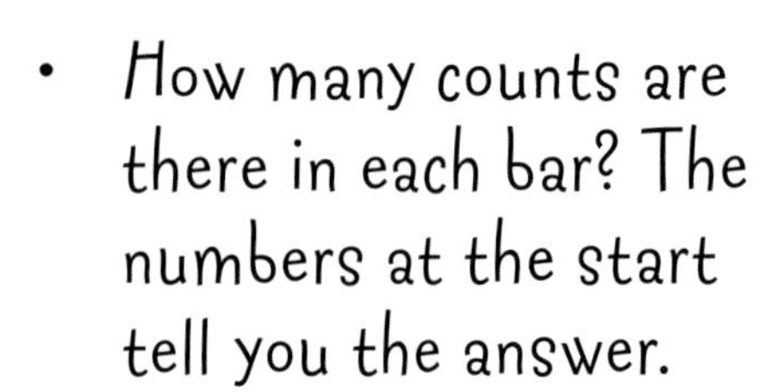

- How many counts are there in each bar? The numbers at the start tell you the answer.

In the tune opposite, you need to count 3 in each bar.

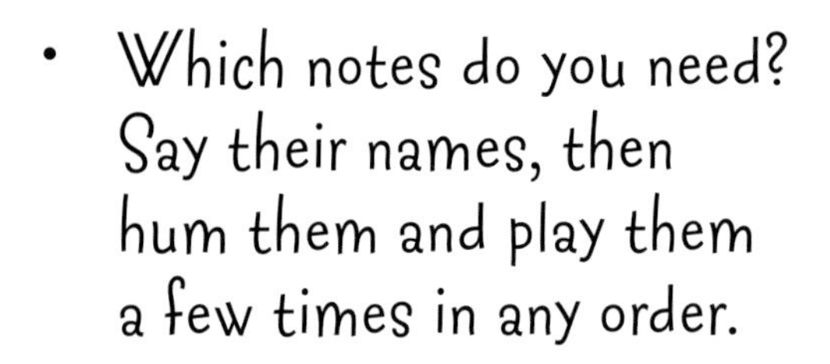

- Which notes do you need? Say their names, then hum them and play them a few times in any order.

In the tune opposite, you need B, A, G, E, and low D.

- Find parts of the music that are repeated. This makes tunes easier to learn.

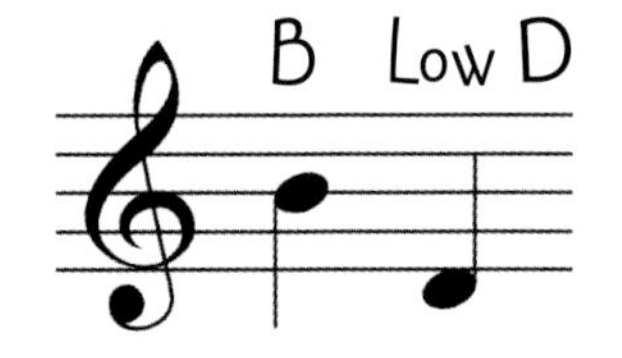

In the tune opposite, you have to play the jump from B down to low D four times.

There's a hole in my bucket

The first two counts of this tune are rests, so start playing on the third count.

If you spot repeated steps and jumps, name the notes, hum them, and play them. This helps you learn the tune. Read more about steps and jumps on page 17.

Another type of dotted note

A dot after a note makes it longer by a half. So a one-count note with a dot lasts one-and-a-half counts. For the music below, hold the first note until you count 'two' and play the second note when you say 'and'.

So this...

...is the same as this.

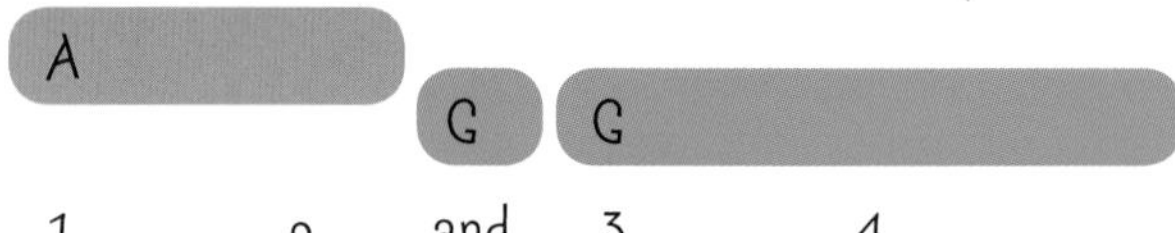

Count 'one, two, three, four' regularly throughout.
Can you find this dotted note in 'Ode to Joy', opposite?

Make up your own tunes

Here are some ideas to help you make up some tunes of your own.

- Play a tune you already know, but change some notes to make a new one.
- Your tune could move up or down by steps or jumps, or stay the same. It's up to you.

- Your name is a pattern of long and short sounds. Can you play notes in that pattern?
- Play your tune a few times until you can remember it. Can you write it down?

Ode to Joy

This tune comes from a big piece of music for voices and instruments. It was written by a man named Beethoven (say 'bay-toe-vun').

If you find some parts of a tune tricky, play them on their own a few times. This helps your fingers learn how to move.

Joining notes together

Sometimes it sounds better to link notes smoothly than to play them separately. A curved line called a slur tells you to do this.

To play a slur, say 'tuh' for the first note but not for the second one. The notes will join up. Make sure you move your fingers neatly.

When to take a breath

Not all music contains signs telling you when to take a breath. Sometimes you have to decide for yourself. Here are some hints.

- A rest is often a good place to breathe.
- If there are no rests, try breathing at the end of a long note.
- It is usually better to breathe at the end of a bar than in the middle.
- Try to breathe in the same places each time you play the tune.

Try to breathe deeply and evenly. If you ever feel dizzy when playing, stop for a while and rest.

Over the hills and far away

Play this tune with and without slurs. Which do you like better? Choosing when and how to play slurs is part of your skill as a recorder player.

Try slurring the notes in groups of four instead of two. Which do you prefer?

Looking after your recorder

Each time you finish playing, wipe your recorder with a clean cloth and put it somewhere safe.

- To clean the inside, you can buy a special cloth called a pull-through.
- Don't leave your recorder in a very cold or very hot place.

Getting better at playing

If you play your recorder as often as possible, your playing will quickly get better. Try to play a little bit every day.

- A music stand like this is a useful place to put your music when you play.

Going further

If you like playing and want to learn more, it is a good idea to find a teacher. A teacher will help you to improve, and to learn new notes and tunes.